TRADING CRYPTOCURRENCIES FOR SENIORS

A Step-by-Step Guide to Trade Cryptocurrencies for Profit and Steps to Avoid Pitfalls

Sean Scott

Copyright

Contents

CHAPTER ONE

HOW MONEY WORKS

Times are changing and the financial world is changing with it. As the world continues to adapt to the endless possibilities of what the digital space offers, many more inventions will continue to unfold. Money as a medium of exchange has become what defines wealth and to a large extent, the pedigree of value and self-worth.

In every sense of the world – the economics aspect of it, most crucially - money defines what revolves around the whole. Arguably, economics is not viewed as acquiring wealth quicker than envisaged but it all boils down to trading things in possession for the things you want; simply referred to as the barter system. While many still resort to this barter system, money is however used for almost all transactions in the world today. In whatever form it is represented, the exchange of money is a more pragmatic and efficient way of doing business.

Economists point out that money serves three main purposes. First, it acts as a form of exchange'. It is generally accepted for payment for goods and services. This indicates that we are not stuck in the barter system. Money can also be used as a unit of account and as a store of value. These also indicate that money can be saved up and used because it is a standardized metric that allows you to measure the relative value of things.

Additionally, there is often the misconception that money comes in the form of coins and cash validated and issued by governments in power. The point is what economists consider money is anything that is accepted as a form of exchange – This has howbeit changed overtime. Today, coins and cash represent money, as they are easy to move around, alongside the fact that they are durable and specially made in ways that are often difficult to counterfeit. However, the view of money has experienced a significant change – It now moves around electronically.

Increasingly, individuals are paid in the form of direct deposits in financial institutions and banks or are issued checks. Money now exists digitally in computers. This is as long as the security of the system is assured and an unlikely event or Trojan attack does not impede. If the monetary system of a nation is kept secured and functions properly as it should, electronic money will do as they are assigned.

A fast growing form of money is which is at the center of this book is cryptocurrency. Cryptocurrencies, particularly the first and most popular kind, Bitcoin is a digital money for the digital age. As against conventional money, Bitcoin is said to be most divisible, most transportable, most verifiable and most recognizable form of money in history.

Cryptocurrencies are virtual currencies that are not issued or regulated by a specific country. Unlike other electronic currency, Bitcoin does not involve a bank, so people can in theory buy things more anonymously. Bitcoin is also more of a speculative asset that allows people to make profit. In hindsight, this limits the use of cryptocurrencies in buying and selling actual goods or services, but investing in this digital currency can secure a lot of profit.

Lately, the cryptocurrency market, particularly Bitcoin, has been experiencing a crucial surge with the release of mind-boggling stimulus packages, the dollar getting inflated, a lot more corporations turning into the side of investments and a whole lot of factors, which will be revealed in this book. In cryptocurrency, a lot of individuals have experienced real time personal successes making hundred thousand dollars.

Often most people find it extremely tedious to attain financial freedom and that has plunged them in a state of lack and want. In the money world, what these individuals lack is indeed financial confidence. This is based on the confidence and acumen to generate money. Most individuals think that there is a money scarcity and making more money is a herculean task. This notion is deeply untrue. In every facet of the economy, money remains unseated but it can only be acquired by those who have the right knowledge and skill to coup it.

Money can be likened to a game of chess, which is strategically played with a number of rules to follow in order to win. You can only become a principal of your financial affairs if you stick to the rules and become a master of them. This is what is going to be opened up to you as we take a walk in the cryptocurrency terrain.

Evolution of Money
Considering money as an abstract of value, it has been represented in diverse forms as something that enables trade or exchange. Since the inception of human civilization, money is reliant on processing ways in which to exchange, tender for, as well as value transfer. From the start, it all kick-started via trade by barter means (transfer of goods for goods). This system was then replaced by standardized token money.

As natural resources that were hard to come by, people began accepting gold and silver universally as choices for money. At that time, they were very apt forms of payment, were the primary form of money for centuries across the globe, and have been instilled in human culture – instinctively as value or wealth. After this, came paper money, which was lighter and easier to carry along in contrast to precious metals.

In the 7th century, China became the first country to adopt this paper form of payment. It was not until the 13th century that the western world began to catch up to this innovation, when it was introduced by Marco Polo to Europe. Even then, the first European banknotes were not issued until the 17th century. Accepting this new paradigm at that time seemed strange and it took several centuries for people to transit from the use of gold and silver coins to banknotes.

Against this backdrop, this led to the birth of the 'gold standard'. The banknotes had no intrinsic value like gold and silver coins; instead they were backed by these precious metals stored in a treasury vault somewhere. The banknotes represented the right to retrieve precious metals from a bank. This was the case until 1944.

Another related system was introduced at the end of the Second World War under the Bretton Woods agreement, tagged the 'gold exchange standard'. This meant that many countries fixed their national currencies' exchange rates to the United States Dollar, which was in turn convertible to gold at a fixed rate. To top that, this convertibility was no longer available to individuals or companies with central banks as the only exception. This system was however terminated in 1971.

Next introduced was the Fiat Currencies, which are extensively still used in today's world. The fiat system refers to when the government assigns value to a currency declaring it a legal tender. This means that a government decides whether a medium of payment will be recognized for financial transactions, trade settlement or commence in a country or jurisdiction.

Some fiat currencies like the US Dollar and the Euro are recognized internationally and used for global trade due to the fact that they are backed by some of the most credible governments and largest economies in the world. To sum up, a fiat currency has value because a government used its power to enforce this value or because exchanging parties agree to its value. Some may even describe this as a collective illusion.

Cryptocurrency became the latest attempt to reinvent the way we exchange money throughout history. Previously, the traditional form of payment had been the only medium to purchasing goods and services. Economists and historians consider cryptocurrency the most important payment invention since gold. Bitcoin began the cryptocurrency revolution when it launched in 2008 but it has several earlier developments that made it possible to revamp the world's currency system.

It was not until the 1980s the technical application of the concept of cryptocurrency came into being. The theory of cryptocurrency was first theorized with the invention of encrypted computer algorithms. This algorithm provided the leeway for cryptocurrency to be exchanged in a secured and irrevocable manner. Through a system called Digicash, units of digital currencies were developed but were only centralized and operated by the company that owned Digicash, founded by David Chaum.

When Digicash went bankrupt, the first working digital currencies; e-gold and PayPal began operations. Inventions like PayPal supported money transfers over the internet and served as a digital alternative to traditional paper methods like checks and money orders. Till this date, PayPal remains a very successful and popular medium of financial exchange in cyberspace.

While both e-gold and PayPal helped facilitate online transactions, they lacked many other characteristics of cryptocurrencies. Cryptocurrency by contrast is a value itself and is also decentralized meaning there is no middleman that coordinates transactions between two parties. Regardless, e-gold and PayPal were both precursors to Bitcoin because they demonstrated the ability to utilize cyberspace to transfer funds and make purchases.

In 1998, a computer scientist, Nick Szabo designed a mechanism for decentralized digital currency using smart contracts, which are digital contracts that cut middlemen using computer supervision. Despite this breakthrough, it took another decade before the idea for cryptocurrency became a reality; enter Bitcoin in 2008.

Although Bitcoin is not the first proposed cryptocurrency, it is notable because it is the first working cryptocurrency. Equally important is the trailblazing record-keeping technology that it introduced to the world – Blockchain. In that year, Satoshi Nakamoto published his white paper, which outlined his vision for the Bitcoin currency in technology. It was Nakamoto who made a proposal for the development of a purely peer-to-peer digital cash system, which would permit individuals to make payments without checks and balances from financial institutions.

Digital Currency vs. Traditional Currency

For many who have jumped ship and stayed on the safety net of the digital currencies, a notable 'advantage' that cryptocurrency has over the conventional currency is that it is deregulated and free from the control of the government or a regulatory body. Neophytes may wonder how possible it is for a currency to be in circulation without some restrictions or control. Well, an intrinsic rule of money is that it must be difficult to produce or retrieve.

Cryptocurrencies like Bitcoin are produced and powered by complex computer algorithms, which as you may guess correctly embodies a lot of computational power to ensure that it stays within a finite supply and is not easily replicated. Additionally, cryptocurrencies are globally accepted with the digital space, meaning that are tied to a single nation or institution. This also means that they are decentralized and recognized worldwide as having worthy values.

One of downsides to traditional currency or fiat currency is that it is not efficient at transferring value across borders. For instance, if you want to send money from the United States to the Caribbean, it may take about three to five business days and also attract additional costs. As such, it becomes too expensive to send a small amount of money that has a huge efficiency of fiat currency and the infrastructure that supports it. This has extremely hampered the efficient flow of traditional currencies, making digital or crypto currencies a much viable option.

Digital assets on the other hand were seen as a response to the financial crisis to the greed of the central banks that could print as much money as they wanted. Cryptocurrencies like Bitcoin are decentralized currencies that are backed by cryptography and governed by a system of code, in contrast to fiat currencies, which are controlled by a central authority. While fiat currencies are reliant on central banks, cryptocurrencies are trustless and reliant on additional edge of technology essentially a network effect.

Cryptocurrency is also scarce and it has varied use cases. While cryptocurrency is still very much in its early stage, it has already given rise to some revolutionary technologies. For example, stable coins, which allow you to tether any real world asset to a digital currency. With this new technology, you are able to transact in a much more fast and efficient manner.

Digital currency has also given rise to decentralized finance where you are able to issue loans without a central authority, as well as a new form of cross border payment system via the use of XRP token, which was created by the ripple company. This has ensured that the time frame for sending currency across borders has sped up, taking up just a few minutes.

While cryptocurrency may have brought a breath of fresh air to those who leverage the space, there are also downsides to the use. One of the negative sides of digital currencies is that there have been many irregularities and illegalities to the how it is been used and distributed, most notably on Initial Coin Offerings (ICOs). This is as a result of the fact that the digital currency space is not as regulated as traditional finance. Similarly to fiat currencies where billions are laundered by corrupt officials and drug dealers, cryptocurrencies are also used for illegitimate purposes like purchase hard, illegal drugs.

Moving from Traditional Investments
Investments in the financial world transcend major boundaries as it gives the leverage to explore diverse means of making money. Prior to the advent of digital or cryptocurrencies, investment portfolios in precious metals, stock markets, bonds, forex and the likes were more popular. Until date, many are diversifying their investments and cryptocurrency has helped elevated these options across several investment platforms.

There is no such thing as investing too much. Neither are there rules that say investment must be streamlined or downsized to one or few portfolios. Individuals who make lots of money in the real world are known for their investment prowess in the short and long terms. However, one must always tread with caution by choosing the right investment portfolio with manageable risks and leeway to breed financial growth. For the cryptocurrency network, it is an investment platform that you can delve into and reap massively even as a beginner.

In diversifying your investment, it is critical that a level of balance is created. Undoubtedly, investment in cryptocurrency is a bespoke way to balance and also step up your portfolio in the financial scheme of things. In no small measure, the cryptocurrency industry differs in every aspect from that which traditional investment stems from and it is fluid and decentralized. Crypto is also a great way to increase your growth in investing and maximize your potential in trading. This stems from the fact that the cryptocurrency market tends to react to global events happening in the financial sphere.

More so, it is becoming glaring that there is a huge growth potential in the cryptocurrency market and more businesses are tilting towards that direction. According to viable records put forward by financial analysts. In 2017 for instance, the cryptocurrency world recorded the biggest investment success when a number of investors practically reaped maximally in millions of dollars. It was said to have been reported by the New York Times and Wall Street Journal.

In essence, it is equally possible to transit from the traditional fiat investment to cryptocurrency investment or stay on track on both sides of the divide. One of the attractive features of investing in Bitcoin is that it can help you gain capital appreciation. Cryptocurrency offers you some of the best advantages similar to the dividends and profit offered in the stock and forex markets respectively.

Currency of the Future

One thing the economic crisis of 2008 has revealed to a lot of investors is how flawed United States traditional banking systems are and this has been confirmed by even the most prominent financial institutions and top investors. More individuals are seeing the need for more sustainable and inexpensive alternatives and that's exactly what crypto offers; a system that is secured, decentralized and free from the clutches of banks and the iron-fisted government.

The most fascinating thing about digital currencies is that even financial institutions are coming to terms with the fact that cryptocurrency is set to displace the conventional means of moving money. In a report by Germany Deutsche bank, it highlighted how traditional money was indeed a fragile system and envisaged that come 2030, more than 200 million people will take advantage of digital money and by then traditional money will be preparing to phase out and most likely and face a possible extinction.

In the same vein, Twitter's Founder, Jack Dorsey, also believes that a foremost cryptocurrency, Bitcoin will ultimately become the world's single currency. Also, Elon Musk the Founder of Tesla and SpaceX revealed that cryptocurrency is a much-enhanced medium to transfer value than a printed paper (fiat currency). With all of these revelations, it is becoming glaring that digital currency is set to take the world by storm and there is every need for you to get abreast with the technology.

The Blockchain technology is the biggest technological invention since the internet came into limelight Just as we rely on the internet for communication it is soon going to be the same for financial transactions using the Blockchain. With Bitcoin and other forms of digital currencies becoming currencies for the present and of the future, you are better positioned for opportunities in this space. You can make or receive payments with a crypto account and save but the really big opportunity comes with investing in crypto. Take Bitcoin for instance, if you had invested $100 five years ago, by now that money would have experienced a huge surge to about $2500.

Additionally, the pioneer of cryptocurrency, the Blockchain network is here to stay. Bitcoin is built on Blockchain the same way that Google revolves around the internet. There are sizable proofs that Blockchain is going to become more important. As it stands big businesses are already harvesting the Blockchain network to record complex data. As such, it is set to become a dominating force in the business domain and companies are already delving in.

Correspondingly, many Fortune 500 companies and other big businesses are keying into the initiative and investing in the crypto space. Many big businesses are already accepting payment and doing business in cryptocurrencies making the digital currency system very worthwhile and acceptable, at least to a considerable length. Although other companies are still reluctant to allow payment in it because it is still volatile, however, that is bound to even out overtime and more businesses will accept cryptocurrencies like Bitcoin as a standard form of payment.

Asides Bitcoin, other cryptocurrencies like Ethereum, Litecoin, Dash, Ripple and Lisk also have huge potentials to grow and bring great returns to savvy investors. To know which coin to invest, you definitely need to get educated and acquire some cryptocurrency experience under your belt.

s

CHAPTER TWO

WHAT IS CRYPTOCURRENCY

In the previous chapter, we highlighted how cryptocurrency has become the currency of the present and one for the future. Although digital money has long been existence with the advent of e-gold and PayPal, however cryptocurrency has revolutionized digital money, making it more people-friendly and free from the throttlehold of bureaucracy. Coupled with the technology behind and how the system works, cryptocurrency aims to solve the fundamental problems associated with making transactions.

While cryptocurrency is yet to fully become standardized, there has been a reasonable amount of acceptance from both the public, business as well as government institutions, particularly in Asia where China invented its own type of cryptocurrency, the Central Bank Digital Currency (CBDC). This highlights the significance of the cryptocurrency and how it is steering a change in the financial space. Cryptocurrency also seeks to curb the inadequacy and inequality of the current financial system.

As credible reports reveal, the number of unbanked and underbanked individuals across the globe has risen to 3 billion people. More so, the current financial system in usual cases, has limited financial freedom, creating intermediaries and brokers in the process.

This has slowed the pace of transactions and has made the process very expensive.

These challenges are what cryptocurrency hopes to solve in short and long terms. However, a proper understanding of what cryptocurrency is and how it works will arm you with the right amount of arsenal to launch your investment and trading motives.

What exactly is Cryptocurrency?
A cryptocurrency primarily functions as a digital asset, which works as a medium of exchange value within a peer-to-peer economic system that uses cryptography to verify and secure transactions and regulate the formation of additional units. As you are aware, the cryptocurrency system does not model the centralized banking systems. Like Bitcoin, most cryptocurrencies such as are decentralized by a circulated network of computers spread around the world, otherwise referred to as nodes.

Cryptocurrencies are easy to distribute as anyone with access to the internet can exchange valuables in any parts of the world just with a single button-click. In contrast to transactions made via intercontinental banks, the cost of transacting cryptocurrencies is minimal and free from strenuous paper works. Additionally, the transactions made via cryptocurrency are irreversible compared to transactions authenticated by companies, which enable credit cards.

The units of cryptocurrency are issued and managed by a network structure based on cryptographic proofs and programmed algorithms. These are regarded as protocols, which set predefined rules that, orchestrate how the system should operate and be managed. In light of this, the decentralization of cryptocurrencies means that the system is not under the control of a single entity. Furthermore, transactions performed are done between two direct parties without the need to rely on a third-party intermediary.

However, many cryptocurrencies are managed and developed by private companies and foundations, meaning that there are changing degrees of centralization. Depending on the node distribution and network architecture, some cryptocurrencies can be considered more centralized than others. The core component for most cryptocurrencies, as earlier emphasized, is the Blockchain technology.

What the Blockchain represents is that it contains a linear chain of multiple linked blocks that are cryptographically secured. Among many of its components, each block in a Blockchain contains a long list of transactions made recently, as well as key references to the block that precedes it. Blockchain is saddled with the responsibility of keeping a permanent record of all complete transactions, working as a decentralized digital ledger. The ledger formed is disbursed across all nodes in the network, thereby fortifying its resistance to any form of alteration.

Bitcoin was earlier introduced as the first decentralized cryptocurrency. The idea behind the influx of Bitcoin was to create an independent and decentralized electronic payment system based on mathematical proofs and cryptography.

As most cryptocurrencies, Bitcoin has a limited supply, which means that Bitcoins will no longer be generated by the system after the maximum supply is reached. Usually, the total supply is public information that is defined when the cryptocurrency is created. While Bitcoin may be the foremost and most popular, there are several other cryptocurrencies, which are keenly taking the space, otherwise known as alternative coins or altcoins. Altcoins all have varying levels of properties and using – all coins, necessarily, do not operate the same.

How Cryptocurrencies Work

The process of gathering cryptocurrencies can be a hard nut to crack for those interested but with no fore knowledge about how it works. Essentially, we have already established that cryptocurrencies are digital monies that are traded online or digitally via the internet and are not based on assets such as gold.

Cryptocurrencies such as Bitcoin, Litecoin, Ethereum and the likes, operate in a completely decentralized system – Blockchain. In subsequent chapters of this book, we will extensively expound on how the Blockchain technology acts as a powerhouse for cryptocurrency and aids in tracking transactions. It works in a way that helps frees users from the threshold of middlemen while eliminating a central record of transactions. However, cryptocurrencies exist as a result of the nodes network and cryptography, which acts as bookkeepers. The intrinsic aspect of cryptocurrency has to do with how transactions are made coupled with how value is added.

To see how this works, let's look at how you make purchase with cryptocurrency:

Take for instance that a book purchase transaction between two individuals is set to occur using Bitcoin, the buyer's choice of cryptocurrency. The buyer begins by logging into their Bitcoin wallet, which is represented by a private key – a unique combination of letters and numbers personalized for each Bitcoin owner.

Like in the case of transactions conducted via financial institutions, currencies get sent to the banks both on the receiving end who keep records of the transactions being conducted, sharing history.

With a traditional financial transaction, the exchanges are sent to banks on each side who record the money being subtracted from one account and added to another. In cryptocurrency transactions, however, recall that the influence of middlemen or banks have been severed. Instead, the buyer's transaction is made visible for public consumption on the Bitcoin's network. These network computers add the buyer's transaction to a list of existing transactions, referred to as a block.

All new transactions made on a block are chained and added to existing blocks on the network, presumably during a 10 minutes window. In addition, a division of the Bitcoin's network gets activated in a bid to solve a very complex and difficult math puzzle in order to ensure that the transactions on the block are verified. When this puzzle is solved, the records of the transactions are confirmed as the official record. Next, the network is allotted a new block on the chain.

These processes are regarded as mining. However, unlike the case of mining golds in rocks, the system digitally solves complex puzzles to provide new coins. This also gives credibility to the network in the sense that no single system can manipulate or monopolize the cryptocurrency market. This is as a result of the many computers which are competing to ensure that a block is verified on the network. Although, many more computers are encouraged to be part of this competition, which makes the puzzle even harder and the competition evenly, timed. For Bitcoin, this process will continue to repeat itself until about 21 million Bitcoins become achievable. Experts have said that this may take up to 2140 before it could be attained.

Bitcoin and Other Cryptocurrencies

At the moment, there are over 2,000 cryptocurrencies available; some of these currencies have gathered enough value in strength, while others are still crawling. Some of the strongest cryptocurrencies include the following:

Bitcoin: Bitcoin is the undeniable leader of cryptocurrencies by far. There are a few reasons Bitcoin tops the lot and it begins with its history and how it broke the ground in altering the course of the financial space. Alongside the Blockchain technology, Bitcoin spearheaded this massive crypto revolution. Bitcoin is the most valuable cryptocurrency because it has the biggest user base.

Created as open source software, Bitcoin permits users to make translucent peer-to-peer transactions, which are visible to all users. However, the algorithm ensures that they are kept under a much-protected condition within the Blockchain. While everyone can see the transaction, the decryption of Bitcoin is left only to the owner by the use of a private key.

Unlike financial institutions such as banks, there are no central authority figures in this network – Bitcoin allows for anonymous transactions globally whereby users regulate the sending and receiving of currencies. As peculiar as it is, Bitcoin is more revered and is offered by more traders as a payment method and has a solid infrastructure due to the Blockchain technology.

Ethereum: Ethereum or Ether, as otherwise known, was launched in 2015. Like Bitcoin, it operates under an open-source network fast-tracked by Blockchain. While it focuses on keeping tabs on the ownership of transactions, Ethereum Blockchain also runs significant codes of decentralized applications, which makes it an ideal network for developing to accelerate fees and service transactions. It has a transaction speed of about 15 seconds.

Ripple: Released in 2012, Ripple runs simultaneously as a digital payment platform for traditional transactions and a cryptocurrency. As a global network, Ripple was created to operate under an efficient, low-cost and more secured method of making transactions. It is unique based and it was designed for speed, stability and reliability. More than that, it is focused on providing one solution: making international payments faster and cheaper, which it does with speeds of mere seconds.

Ripple also permits the exchange of any currency from US dollars, Bitcoin, Gold and Euro. It connects to banks unlike other currencies. Unlike other digital currencies, Ripple's main focus is to move money on a larger scale rather than on a peer-to-peer basis.

Litecoin: A close associate of Bitcoin, Litecoin was in 2011 launched as an alternative to Bitcoin. It operates under an open source and a global network that is utterly decentralized, meaning it is not held bound by protocols from central authorities. In contrast to Bitcoin, Litecoin is believed to feature faster transaction times. The coin limit for Bitcoin is 21 million, whereas the coin limit for Litecoin is 84 million. They operate on different algorithms. Litecoin has a transaction speed of about 3 minutes, which is a lot faster than Bitcoin and the fees are also a lot less than that of Bitcoin.

Bitcoin Cash: Next is Bitcoin cash, which is forked off from Bitcoin in order to make improvements, which it certainly did in terms of transaction speed. Bitcoin cash was formed in order to improve on the feature that Bitcoin was lacking. It increased the size of blocks allowing more transactions to be processed faster, which is under 3 minutes, as well as lowered fees.

Zcash: Zcash as a digital currency was created out of the code-base of Bitcoin and built on a decentralized Blockchain. A core feature in the differentiation of Zcash is the emphasis on privacy. With Zcash, users are able to send and receive money without public notice of the parties linked to the transactions or the amount involved.

Why Cryptocurrency?
Accessible and Ease of Use

One of the great gains of cryptocurrency is that it gives leverage to just about anyone to own and trade. Anyone with an internet, a smartphone or a computer can send and receive cryptocurrency. This is especially beneficial to the unbanked members of the society – people who lack access to traditional banking systems or methods.

Additionally, with traditional systems, you are bound to encounter the obstacles of excessive fees, paperwork, legalese and ill-fated bureaucracy. These hindrances are undoubtedly hectic. Howbeit, with cryptocurrency, these shortcomings have all been nipped in the bud as a result of the peer-to-peer network structure which makes it easy to deal directly with the party you are conducting a transaction with.

Also, due to the fact that cryptocurrency is a decentralized system there are no third party approvals needed for transactions to be rendered successful. Therefore, cryptocurrency transactions are incredibly quick and in many cases instantaneous.

Elimination of Middlemen

A significant advantage of cryptocurrency that many are attuned to is the assurance of lower transaction fees and the elimination of bank charges. In traditional business dealings, middlemen like banks, brokers and agents typically charge varying fees when you perform trades or transactions. These fees range may include processing fees, convenience fees, maintenance fees, annual fees and the likes.

However, since cryptocurrency transactions are one-to-one dealings that occur on a peer-to-peer network structure, it means that the middlemen are taken out of the equation.

More importantly, the transaction fees are greatly reduced or eliminated. Likely exceptions to this, however, are the use of third-party services such as Luno to maintain a cryptocurrency wallet. Compared to the traditional banking systems, these fees are at reduced rates.

More Secured Transactions

In most traditional financial systems, information regarding financial activities is made available to third parties when you perform certain transactions. For instance, when you give a merchant your credit card to make payment they are given access to your entire credit line. Additionally, financial institutions record transactions performed and that is not exactly ideal for individuals who may want to have a certain level of privacy.

Credit cards operate a system known as a pull system, while cryptocurrency operates on a push system. The latter means that when a cryptocurrency holder makes a payment or transfer, they only push the information that is relevant to that specific transaction, making a holder less prone to identity theft. This way cryptocurrency ensures personal leverage over transactions and more protection.

Less Transaction Fees for International Payments

Traditional wire transfers and international purchases usually attract certain fees and charges. However, since the advent of cryptocurrency, which have excluded intermediary institutions, the cost of transactions between a user in one country and a user across borders are kept significantly low. This is especially beneficial to frequent international travelers.

Gaining Financial Security

Cryptocurrency presents the best opportunity to escape financial obscurity. With the surging inflation and debt in different countries of the globe, it has become crucial to protect your financial future in the best way possible. One of the shocking statistics to come out of the banking system is the amount of debt that most Americans owe on credit cards.

This circumstance, as the world grapples with inflation, is becoming increasingly difficult to fix. On the bright side, those who are keen on gaining financial security on the short and long term, are tilting towards cryptocurrency trading. Cryptocurrency provides you with a bespoke investment portfolio to secure your future financially.

This significant aspect of cryptocurrency has to do trading, which involves speculating the movements of the prices of coins through trading accounts. On the other hand, gains can also be made by exchange (buying and selling) underlying coins in positions. The source of return in cryptocurrency trading is the price increase of the coins determined by supply and demand. The aim is to allow the price to increase overtime and then trade it. These acts, if studied to perfections, can help you diversify your assets and give you the much-needed financial freedom. Cryptocurrency if utilized effectively can help supplement your current assets, based on returns and risks.

Financial security means that you are intentional about how you spend your money and build enough strategic investment to give you return and build up your wealth in the short and long term. This also means structuring and gaining control over your finances so that they work for you, accumulating overtime and keeping you feeling secured. The goal here is to stop depending solely on your salary as a source of income and have more freedom on how to spend your finances.

For most individuals holding different currencies (USD, Euros, and Pounds Sterling) at their disposal sheds light on ways to kick off this process. Holding cryptocurrency is no different in this regard, as it is getting more integrated into our lives. While cryptocurrencies are versatile and cyclical, their value tends to increase overtime as they are getting accepted more rapidly. As a way to diversify your portfolio, cryptocurrency comes in handy, but you should be saddled to stay in it for the long haul. Of course, there would be hiccups and volatility throughout that journey, but if you are ready to stay in it for the long term, the value would experience a significant rise.

Seeing that the mass adoption of cryptocurrency is about to get into full gear is a testament to the fact that it's worth will only increase in value. Undoubtedly, diversifying your investment and creating your cryptocurrency portfolio is a vital step towards the right direction. Correspondingly, cryptocurrency investment grants you the leeway to earn more passive income. Logically as is with stocks and bonds, you can get passive income and returns on your investment, and sometimes even more than the regular investment. Although, as it becomes more risky, the returns get even higher.

On the flipside, many have argued that cryptocurrency will not automatically turn you into a millionaire. While there is an element of truth in this disposition, the key is to be savvy and confident in your investments. Considering the risks involved, you will be armed with the right techniques and strategies to make the most of cryptocurrency trading as will go further in this guide.

Getting Started – Things You Should Know

Whether you see cryptocurrency has a way of building your investment portfolio or an easier means for running transactions, you should not go in blind. Understanding the perks as well as the risks associated with cryptocurrency is a pertinent demand that you should succumb to if you must succeed in your investment. While you have made the decision to get rid of the fiat and embrace the world of cryptocurrency trading, there are certain principles that you need to get abreast with before delving in.

Set a Trading or Investing Motive

The cryptocurrency market is wild space harnessed by a lot of individuals you can call the large whales. These are thousands of Bitcoin harvesters and traders who wait patiently for the right moment to strike before acquiring what they keenly set for themselves. This highlights the importance of having a clear motive about what you want from the cryptocurrency space. Trade cryptocurrency comes with a certain realization that your winnings will be corresponded with losses as well. As a digital currency trader, you should be intentional about what you want from the market and not lose sight of key specifics.

It is important to not lose sight of your motive behind trading. Whether your purpose for the market is to trade, scalp or save your currency, you must ensure that this motive is kept in mind and avoid falling off the rail. This requires optimum patience and solitude; there are days when the tide could turn against you. Every trade you engage in requires that you know when to opt out whether the trade is profiting or not. For instance, if you have set a target for a $1000 profit and you have achieved that on a certain trade, it is advisable to leave and avoid being greedy. The same also applies to loss; you should learn to establish a stop loss level and count your losses on a reasonable scale.

Cryptocurrency is Volatile

Like the proverbial "Not all that glitters are gold", cryptocurrency is not a get rich quick scheme. A good number of cryptocurrency traders mistake the market for a scheme that could turn them into millionaires overnight. Experienced traders understand that there is a high level of risk involved in the cryptocurrency space and this is determined by its volatility. While there is software that aids in analyzing price trends, they are also not very definite. In a nutshell, you should trade with what you can afford to lose.

The volatility of cryptocurrency is due to the fact that it is still an emerging market with a lot of swings. While many have made millions through cryptocurrency overtime, others have experienced huge losses of investment. The high volatility is often backed by sudden market downturns. For instance, 2017 saw the value of Bitcoin grapple between $900 and $20,000, very much to the detriment of crypto traders. This highlights the fact that cryptocurrency trading is not only volatile but highly risky. It is safer when you try to analyze and comprehend the factors influencing the price of cryptocurrency and use them advantageously.

No fixed Return Rates

A vital point of note in the digital currency space is that there is no definite pattern to the rise and fall in the value of cryptocurrencies. This is due to the absence of regulatory standards and the number of traders harnessing the space. Unlike stock mutual funds, it is wishful thinking to entirely predicate the changes in the value of cryptocurrency or calculate returns. The absence of enough data or credibility also plays a critical role in this. Crypto technologies are still developing and deciphering ways to offer more opportunities in the market.

Whether you are looking into short-term trading or a long-term plan, understand that you will always be prone to uncertainties as you trade or invest. For those looking to make high percentage gains, short-term investments may be ideal as they offer really good opportunities especially when the value of cryptocurrency is experiencing a favorable surge. Also, note that there are side effects to this, particularly as the cryptocurrency market is volatile and prices change with seconds. Long-term plan, on the other hand, is not a complex tactic as you are looking to safe-keep and grow your crypto. However, you miss the opportunity to make short-time gains with prompt changes in value.

CHAPTER THREE

CRYPTOCURRENCY TRADE AND INVESTMENT

In the grand scheme of things, you are either trading cryptocurrency or investing in cryptocurrency. Understanding these two distinct but much-related concepts in the digital financial world will further broaden your horizon and arm you with credible arsenals to raid the cryptocurrency space for desired profit. There is a thin line between trading and investing when evaluating the crypto market. Cryptocurrency is a volatile asset and as such, many investors and traders often target accumulating cryptos such as Bitcoin or making profits in USD.

Firstly, it is pertinent to understand that the motive behind trading and investing are two separate actions in the crypto market. In economics, **trading** is an exchange that occurs when you buy or sell off assets. Assets can be anything of value as long as it can be paid for. However, in the financial markets, traded assets are regarded as financial instruments, which may include fiat or cryptocurrencies, bonds, stocks, margin products, futures and the likes.

On the other hand, **investing** involves the allocation of resources to a certain course with the aim of generating profit. For instance, a capital could be used to fund a business or buy an asset with the sole purpose of reselling at a higher price. Typically, in the financial market, financial instruments are invested on and resold at a higher price – an expectation referred to as 'Return on Investment' (ROI).

While the motive behind trading and investing is to generate profit, the key difference here, particularly in the financial markets, is the strategy or technique applied to achieve the intended profit-making objective. Traders of cryptocurrency often target short-term returns as they tend to exploit or capitalize on the volatility of the market. In the cryptocurrency market, traders are analytical in their approach as they study trends and make multiple trades frequently.

Investors are more profit-oriented on a long-term basis, which may span over a period of months, years or even decades. Investing in the cryptocurrency market takes a lot of patience as many investors often HODL their cryptos – a term which refers to not selling your cryptocurrency to allow it generate more value. In a nutshell, investors see cryptocurrencies like Bitcoin as a store of value which could give massive returns in the near future.

Your decision as a trader or investor is largely dependent on how well you understand the market trends and cycles, volatility and vulnerability. Market trends are movement of the prices of assets in the crypto. As an investor and particularly an investor, it is crucial to recognize these trends, identify them at their most beneficial moment and use them to your advantage. On a crypto chart, you will notice these trends marked out by green and red lines as well as price actions. Common terms given to these markets are bull and bear, which are used to identify the upward or downward movement of the market. The Bull market refers to a sustained upward trend where the prices of assets are constantly scaling. On the flipside, the Bear market relays a sustained downward trend where the prices of assets are constantly sloping.

For cryptocurrencies such as Bitcoin, it has continued to experience a Bull trend since it emerged fully in 2009. However, a sustained bull market can also have a bear trend in between at different times, and vice versa.

This means that there is every possibility that a market trend will rise and fall regardless of its sustained overall movement, which is simply natural, as more people tend to exploit the cryptocurrency market.

Another vital aspect of the cryptocurrency market that traders look forward to when studying assets is what is regarded as market cycle. This means that the market portrays a certain trend or pattern at intervals.

Cryptocurrency as Tradable Assets

Anyone who has been involved in the purchase of any form of cryptocurrency has done the basic in performing a very simple trade. However, this action could be regarded as barely scratching the surface of the crypto market and the amount of options available. In this guide, you will be instructed on the specifics on making your first crypto trade and explore some of the more advanced aspects of the process.

The first trade almost everyone makes is the fiat to crypto trade. Brokers and Exchanges such as Luno, Binance, act as an on-ramp for users into the space depending on location and jurisdiction. These exchanges sell cryptocurrency for a variety of fiat currencies. It is very pertinent that you do your research into the most reputable exchanges available in your area. Some things you should keep in mind are the exchange's reputation, their fee structures and their security. Essentially, make sure you are aware of any fees the exchange will take from your transactions and how they will keep your funds secure. A more incisive look on the best exchanges and brokers to use will be taken in the next section.

Once your funding has been verified on an exchange platform, you can make your trade for whatever cryptocurrency the exchange offers. The most popular coins such as Bitcoin, Ethereum, Ripple, Litecoin, are often more domineering on these exchange platforms. Once your trade from the fiat to cryptocurrency has been made, you are now set to activate your crypto. Behind the scenes the exchange will have created a wallet for you where your funds are stored. You will have to make a decision to either keep the funds on the exchange or move them elsewhere. In the crypto space, there are two kinds of wallet that you can own – Hot wallet or Cold storage.

A hot wallet can be likened to the wallet you carry on a daily basis. It is not particularly safe but it is convenient and grants you easy access to your funds. A critical example of the hot wallet is the cryptocurrency exchange. It is a software wallet that is always available to use online and requires password input to access. This makes it technically vulnerable to cyber-attacks, however, it also makes it easy to reach your money.

Contrastingly, cold storage can be regarded as a savings account, which is not mobile in real time but is more secure and impractical to use at will. The cold storage models a piece of hardware that is separate from your computer. It is always offline, except for when you plug it in to access it. This means that the wallet is offline and is totally safe from cyber attackers or hackers. The emphasis on the kind of wallet to use depends on your decision to use your cryptocurrency frequently or lock them away. It is advisable to pick a wallet that is most appropriate to you.

Whatever wallet you opt for, you will be provided with a public key and a private key. The public key is the address that you will always use to receive funds. When you withdraw from an exchange and you are required to provide an address, the public key is the one to tender. The public key is made public for all to see and you are at liberty to share it and use in any mode you choose. On the other hand, the private key should never under any circumstances be shared. If your private key is leaked or discovered then your funds can be stolen and used without your permission or input. Your funds may be lost and may not be recovered. Exchanges operate under strict policies that require you to keep your private safe from prying eyes.

1A1zP1eP5QGefi2DMPTfTL5SLmv7DivfNa

The above is a cryptocurrency (Bitcoin) address believed to be owned by the inventor of Bitcoin, Satoshi Nakamoto

Once you have your cryptocurrency stored in the most appropriate place, you are set up to engage in crypto-to-crypto trades. These work similarly as fiats to crypto trades but you are working within the Blockchain ecosystem. This translates to taking whatever cryptocurrency you purchased with your fiat and trade it directly for another cryptocurrency. For instance, you can trade Bitcoin for Ethereum or vice versa.

There are many exchanges that offer these services. Note that many of these exchanges are centralized while others are not. Ensure that you look into the exchanges history and security to ensure that you are comfortable with who you are dealing with. With these trades available as well as some practice and research for more reputable service providers, you are well set up to purchase and trade for any cryptocurrency you keenly desire.

Cryptocurrency Brokers and Exchanges
From inception, we have emphasized on how cryptocurrency operates a decentralized system devoid of checkmates and authorization from a central institution or the government. However, they are

companies who stand in the gap regarding the procurement and trading of cryptocurrencies. We earlier referred to these seeming intermediaries as Exchanges or Brokers. Although you may find traditional cryptocurrency exchanges worthwhile, however, some of the best and most trusted exchanges often operate digitally.

Before we take a deep into the use of brokers and exchanges, the traditional means of getting cryptocurrencies also comes into play. For instance, if you are keen on trading cryptocurrencies and do not want to go through exchanges, you can activate the peer-to-peer method. This entails paying cash for cryptocurrency through a friend or trusted associate. More often than not, there are cryptocurrency holders, often regarded as brokers, with enough assets who are willing to sell off their assets at the right price. Meanwhile, the digital medium is most advisable as they can be relied upon for seamless transactions.

Cryptocurrency exchanges are digital platforms or certified websites where you can initiate the trade or exchange of cryptocurrency for fiat currencies or digital currencies. In these exchanges, crypto buyers and sellers also conduct their businesses. For instance, when a deposit is made on a Bitcoin address on the exchange, the holder can sell his Bitcoin for Dollars or an alternative coin with the positive balance. In the same vein, a Bitcoin buyer will also have to deposit their Dollars with the exchange to initiate a buy with the balance. Real exchanges are really just a medium between traders.

Getting your hand on the most prospective digital assets of cryptocurrency may involve a lot of process due to the fact that changes in regulations and acceptance occur overtime. However, this is also tied to your trading or investing objectives and what you hope to achieve financially in the short and long run. Regardless, your journey in the crypto world begins by getting a wallet.

As emphasized briefly earlier, a crypto wallet is where you store your digital assets or cryptocurrency. Your wallet is what sustains your crypto and whatever transaction you choose to make. Since cryptocurrencies are not stored in banks, you would have to go through digital exchanges to create a wallet of your own. In real sense, Cryptocurrency wallets are programs that help you manage your digital currencies. Fiat currencies can be exchanged as cryptocurrencies and stored in wallets on an exchange. Since cryptocurrencies are not physical like fiat, this emphasizes the importance of getting a crypto wallet if you ever want to get your crypto journey started.

Technically, a crypto wallet does not actually store your cryptocurrency but they host your wallet addresses or keys, which are like access to your currency. Every crypto trader or investor has a unique wallet address, meaning no two individuals will ever possess the same keys. When an exchange of cryptocurrency is made, the sender completely hands off the currency to your wallet address. There also must be a match between the private key and public address in order to use the crypto that was assigned. Generally, all transactions are signified and recorded by the Blockchain technology.

Popular Digital Currency Exchanges (DCE)
There are many different types of exchanges available and there also brokers (as mentioned earlier) on the other hand, who own cryptocurrencies and sell from their ownerships. Brokers usually sell at market prices, which are a lot higher. However, the

fact is that if you can invest more, you should find the lowest price and the best exchange to buy from, due to the fact that these exchanges are not wired together. There are also different prices at different exchanges.

More importantly, these exchanges have different modes of operations. There are exchanges that are only focused on trading cryptocurrencies for other digital currencies, while others help exchange digital currencies for cash. Generally, exchanges often come in two forms namely; Centralized Cryptocurrency Exchange (CEX) and Decentralized Cryptocurrency Exchange (DEX). The former can be likened to traditional stock exchanges where buyers and sellers agree on a trade and the exchanges acts as an intermediary. During this process, a commission is charged by the exchange to facilitate the transactions. The latter, on the other hand, is solely a pure cryptocurrency operation that runs transactions without the aid of an intermediary or middleman. In this exchange, the buyers and sellers transact directly with one another in a peer-to-peer. This is also where the term 'smart contracts' were coined. A smart contract is an agreement executed between a seller and a buyer, written into lines of code.

Some of the most popular Centralized Cryptocurrency Exchange (CEX) includes the following:

- **Coinbase**

- **Binance**

- **Bittrex**

- **Kucoin**

- **Kraken**

- **Roqqu**

- **Gemini**

Some of the most Decentralized Cryptocurrency Exchange (DEX) includes the following:

- **Stellar DEX**

- **Bisq DEX**

- **IDEX**

- **Wave DEX**

Pertinently, there are three things to look out for or consider before joining an exchange and these include:

Status: It is important that you go through reviews from crypto users and renowned websites on a crypto exchange platform before using them. Take time to conduct your survey on the best possible platform and ask lots of questions on the deliveries.

Rates: When you go through most of the exchange platforms, they provide details on the fees and rates they charge on digital currencies. Ensure that you retrieve pertinent information or their fees including transaction, deposits and withdrawal. Not all exchanges run the same framework.

Payment Methods: This is a very vital point to note while searching for a viable and credible crypto exchange. Understand the payment method available to an exchange before delving in. Ask questions on what methods they use, including credit and debit cards, transfer types, PayPal usage and most importantly the payment options available to the website and your country. Also, most exchanges require identity verifications before making trade and this often comes with much higher rates.

Blockchain Technology

It cannot be gainsaid or emphasized enough that Blockchain Technology is at the heart of digital currencies. It is an automated database that facilitates a network of distributed ledger technologies. Blockchain acts as an innovation solution to the challenges bedeviling individuals as regards centralization. This technology helps store records of transactions, stumbling checks from central authorities. Blockchain is impossible to fiddle and it creates a bespoke way of maintaining a ledger in a decentralized form. It is also considered to have the potential to drive more businesses

The Blockchain is a database or digital ledger of transactions but this database differs from traditional databases. In a traditional database, data is stored on a centralized server with a single authority empowered to change or delete the data. In Blockchain the data is shared across computers that all run on software that keeps identities of data intact.

Data in Blockchain is secured through cryptography and can only be altered by people authorized to do so. Before we delve into how the Blockchain technology works, we would start by comprehending what a block is. A block is a piece of information that is made of data. The block contains a timestamp, which is used to create what is called the hash of the block. The block also has the hash of the previous block. There are various kinds of data that can be stored in a block. The data can be related to medical records, election information, smart contracts or land records.

The hash is the unique identity of a block, much like the fingerprint of a human being, every block also contains the hash of the previous block. This is what creates a chain of interconnected blocks and gives this technology its unique name. Every time a new block is added, a time stamp is added to all the transactions.

How Does Blockchain Work?
Take for instance, a buyer who is keen on buying a house. When the buyer acquires the house, the seller has to sign a document, which indicates that the buyer now owns the house. In the same vein, the seller also has to provide proof that when the house was bought, the previous owner also signed a similar document granting ownership of the house. In essence, the house has to have

proof of the chain of ownership all the way to the beginning.

Blockchain can be highlighted in the same vein as the scenario started. For each unit of the chain, there is a cryptographically verifiable chain of the history of ownership. In Blockchain the registry id is distributed to everybody. This means that anyone can verify at any time how many units are in circulation, who owns them and what the history of their ownership is.

Transactions are not just verified by one single authority but by the consensus of multiple users. Since information is stored across networks of computers, it makes it very hard for anyone to manipulate or delete the data without calling on the attention of others on the network. As A result, the Blockchain helps to validate and protect sensitive information such that trust is established. It can also help to reduce costs, improve speed and enhance productivity.

Cryptocurrency and Blockchain Interactions Cryptocurrency is an ever-evolving industry with new technologies and ways to interact with the Blockchain. There has been a lot of misconception about the Blockchain technology, what it does and most conspicuously, its relationship with cryptocurrencies. One of the many wrong ideas developed out there is that Blockchain is a cryptocurrency on its own, especially when compared to Bitcoin. This is not only false but very misleading in your sense of purpose. Again, cryptocurrencies such as Bitcoin are digital monies, which are kept on their feet by the Blockchain technology. Asides this duty, Blockchain also solves a number of pertinent challenges for other financial organizations in terms of storing large data.

Blockchain and Bitcoin (being the first cryptocurrency developed) are often interchangeably used because they are closely related, but they refer to two distinct things. Bitcoin is the first ever application on Blockchain, perhaps that is why so many people equate it with the Blockchain technology that powers it. Nonetheless, it is only one of the cryptocurrencies that Blockchain powers, including Ethereum, Litecoin, Dash, Monero, which are also very popular.

The Blockchain technology is often likened to the internet of the 90s due to its revolutionary entry into the digital world. It is an incorruptible system for recording transactions that is open, verifiable and yet secure. It is used to trade cryptocurrencies like Bitcoin and for other purposes like maintaining voting records or medical data. Blockchain is secure because it does not record transactions at one central point, which can easily be hacked. It uses a distributed system for verification that checks itself at regular intervals to maintain consensus on records.

Further described as the internet of value, Blockchain eliminates all intermediaries in cryptocurrency transactions and is used for purposes like exchanging assets online through smart contracts, making peer-to-peer payments in sharing economy crowdsourcing venture capital funds , making regulations transparent in governance and for verifying the history of things in supply chain auditing. The application of Blockchain has proven that it is durable, robust and transparent. It is indeed a ground-breaking technology that has the ability to transform our digital future.

CHAPTER FOUR

ULTIMATE BITCOIN GUIDE

Bitcoin is an unregulated digital currency system that allows you to transfer assets across the globe utilizing the Blockchain technology. In other words, it is a decentralized electronic payment system. As well-known, the technology was invented by the enigmatic Satoshi Nakamoto whose identity has remained a secret since the technology's invention in 2008. Bitcoin is a highly secure peer-to-peer network that uses a distributed ledger management system that is both transparent and secure.

Bitcoin was invented with the vision to eliminate third-party intermediaries like governments and brokers from online transactions to create a system of economy and trade, which is undoubtedly one for the future. Bitcoin is legitimate and immutable as it tackles issues of currency manipulation and loose banking systems and can even be exchanged for real money. It is no wonder that the currency's price has skyrocketed in recent times, especially since it borrows features from Blockchain.

In simple terms, Bitcoin is not regulated in the traditional sense of some currencies or investments but that does not mean it is free for all. Bitcoin operates under an open source and decentralized network, therefore trust is guaranteed. The details of Bitcoin, including transactions, are made available to everyone and go through a transparent method void of discrepancy. Bitcoin payments do not rely on third parties to be made and most importantly, it is protected by cryptographic algorithms. No one person can control Bitcoin, which means that even if there is a shady element in its uses, there are plenty of regular checks that prevent it from going unnoticed.

Like other cryptocurrencies or most, Bitcoin is a cryptocurrency that is based on a decentralized and trustless verification system. To achieve a system that is trustless and fraud proof, Bitcoin operates using cryptography. The Bitcoin philosophy is chiefly nothing more than a public ledger minus trust plus cryptography. This also accentuates the use of the digital signature, which is the Public and Private keys.

As a credible store of wealth, Bitcoin has risen up the ranks as deflationary currency, even as the fiat currency continues to experience a drastic rise in inflation. In the similar mode as gold, the foremost digital currency has the potential to become impeccable in value in times of an economic crisis.   Although, Bitcoin still has a lot to accomplish in terms of its non-perishability and not depreciating as goes on.

There are often myths passed around as regards the legality of Bitcoin. This is what terrifies most beginners who are yet to grasp how the currency works and what backs it. We often hear many individuals echo the thought that Bitcoin is fraudulent because it does not stay within the control of the government. This myth is definitely untrue. Bitcoin is legal and is not a fraudulent currency.

In most countries, Bitcoin is completely legal. However, countries such as Argentina and Russia have very strict bans on foreign and in these countries, Bitcoin is illegal. In other countries like Thailand, for instance, the government limits the licensing of entities like Bitcoin exchanges, which makes it extremely difficult for the currency to succeed. Regardless of these constraints, Bitcoin has a potential to thrive as more countries come to accept its use.

As the use of Bitcoin grows, each country has a responsibility to provide its own regulations and rules on how individuals and businesses should use the new technology. Significantly, they will also provide rules on how it will integrate with their traditional finance systems. In the US, within the United

States Treasury Department, is a body known as the financial crimes enforcement network. This Bureau issued non-binding guidance on the characterization of certain activities involving virtual currencies. This kind of guideline and guidance will help cryptocurrencies be recognized and used more transparently for financial activities.

People often think that Bitcoin is a complicated scheme. While most people would argue that Bitcoin is indeed complicated, the truth is, it is just as complicated the same way as your car or the phone you own. Of course, it requires a degree of technical experience to build a car or a cellphone, but you do not need to possess this knowledge to use or own one; the exact principle goes for Bitcoin. You do not need to be a Bitcoin miner or be able to code to own the currency. Since Bitcoin is a new concept, there is a natural curiosity to know how it works and a healthy mindset in it.

Now you may begin to wonder why the emphasis on Bitcoin is huge when there hundreds of cryptocurrencies available. Bitcoin has been gaining traction because it opened the entry points for other cryptocurrencies to thrive.

How Does Bitcoin Work?
The smallest unit of Bitcoin is one transaction, which in some way, models the fiat currency such as Dollars. For instance, if you want to transfer two Bitcoins to an associate or business collaborator, it would read that you sent that certain amount of Bitcoin to my associate. The challenge with this is that the transaction becomes too transparent to the public. In this light, to protect the identities of users, Bitcoin replaces names with encrypted strings

(Bitcoin address) which take a whole lot of technology to set up.

These values are derived from your public key and are unique to you. It is a difficult task to link these strings to the actual holder except in cases where law enforcers are involved. For these reasons, Bitcoin transactions are considered pseudo anonymous, which means they are not fully anonymous. The next step in having a successful transaction is when the sender appends a signature to the transaction. The math behind it is a bit complicated and relies on an algorithm called SHA256. To sign a transaction, the sender combines the message with the private key and then passes it through the algorithm (SHA256). The output is a signature with a fixed length – 256 bits to be exact.

What makes this algorithm an impressive system is the fact that it is not a reversible function. This means that if the transaction message is known, you cannot find a private key. As previously noted, public keys are used to replace names of individuals with encrypted strings, which are unique like our fingerprints. The sender passes the transaction message and private key into the SHA256 algorithm to generate the signature.

To ensure a transparent system, the transaction is broadcasted to the public so the whole cryptocurrency space is up to date. But how do we verify that the transaction is legitimate? Here, the receiver gets a message that includes the sender's signature and they already are granted access to the sender's public key. After all, it is for the public domain. The key matched and ran against a different algorithm, which generates a true or false tender to determine its validity or authenticity.

Moving forward, the protocol checks the sender's previous transaction history to confirm if the sender has enough Bitcoin to initiate the transaction. To put this in lighter terms, if you want to purchase an automobile that costs $20,000, the seller needs to ensure that you already earned at least that exact amount or more. It is somewhat similar to a credit card check.

Now take for instance that the transaction is valid and verified by all the players, the next significant step is how the transaction would be recorded in the public ledger. Basically, the transaction is not getting lost in space. This is where Blockchain technology comes in. Instead of having a full ledger, we divide it into blocks. Each block lists around 2400 valid transactions and these blocks are interconnected with timestamps.

Blockchain in this process is nothing more than a chain of blocks, one after another. It holds the history of all transactions and everyone in the network has a copy of the recent version. It is for this reason that Bitcoin is regarded as decentralized.

Mining Cryptocurrencies - Bitcoin Mining
In your little research of cryptocurrency, you have probably heard of the word "mining" being associated with digital currency. Naturally, resources such as gold, diamonds, sapphire, and the likes are mined underground. Mining in the cryptocurrency space is done differently, of course digitally, through the use of high performing computers. Personal CPUs were earlier used for Bitcoin mining, before improvement was made in the cryptographic industry with the use of Graphics Processing Units (GPUs).

Cryptocurrency mining is the process whereby new cryptocurrencies such as Bitcoin are produced. This process is actively done by solving computational and mathematical puzzles in order to add transactions to the Blockchain network. It is the digital process in which transactions between users are verified and added to the Blockchain. When a user wants to send a payment or in some cases an item or service to another user, it requires solving a complex equation. These equations are then solved by diverse computer hardware known as miners; at least this is one purpose and form of mining.

A coin that can be mined is known as a proof of work coin. This is a term used in opposition of proof of stake where transactions are validated by stakeholders. Stakeholders in this case are people who own a certain amount of Bitcoin and lock it in a wallet to validate transactions. While proof of stake is becoming more viable thanks to advances in technology, it is generally considered more vulnerable to what is known as a 51% attack. A 51% attack can be executed when a validator owns more than 50% of a total value of Bitcoin. This does not mean, however, that the proof-of-work coins or mining is not vulnerable as well. A mineable coin can suffer a 51% attack if someone controls more than 50% of the hash power.

The hash power, otherwise known as hash rate, is a measurement of the mining hardware's ability to complete equations. More exciting than that, is also the measurement of how much money a miner can potentially earn. The two most important metrics for mining are hash power and power consumption measured in watts. Mining hardware requires power and power costs money. Depending on the miner's choice, this cost can be upfront in the case of solar or recurring in the case of buying from their power company. Either way, the goal is to keep your watts low and your hash rate high. Before investing into mining, you want to calculate both of these metrics.

Mining Hardware

Currently, there are four types of mining hardware namely: ASICS, GPU, CPU, and more recently FPGA.

ASICS: This stands for Application-Specific Integrated Circuit. They are developed for a specific algorithm. Think of the algorithm as the language used to communicate between the miner and the Blockchain. The most popular cryptocurrency mined with ASICS is Bitcoin. This mining hardware is typically the most efficient use of power versus hash rate. However, ASICS presents unique challenges for miners. For instance, ASICS will only mine one algorithm, meaning if the particular algorithm changes, the hardware becomes useless. Additionally, ASICS have no resale value, meaning when upgrading hardware, in most cases, the miner will not be able to recoup any cost of the hardware. Finally, ASICS are primarily manufactured by one supplier. This presents a unique problem for both miners and the coin. For miners, availability comes after the supplier has filled their farms and for the coin presents a possible vulnerability in the form of the aforementioned 51% attack.

GPU: Graphics Processing Units have multiple uses outside of mining and that include content creation, artificial intelligence and gaming. As such, GPUs have multiple manufacturers and larger availability to the public. The most popular cryptocurrency mined with GPUs is Ethereum. GPU mining supports multiple algorithms, meaning if the coin you are mining fails or becomes unprofitable, you can move to another coin. Additionally when upgrading hardware, the miner's old hardware has resale value on the consumer market. The downside of GPU mining includes the need for additional hardware and software along with a constantly moving market to stay educated on.

CPU: The Central Processing Unit is used in almost all technological applications in the world today. This means that there are multiple manufacturers and greater consumer availability. The most popular coined mined by CPU is Monero. CPU mining like GPU mining supports multiple algorithms. However, CPU mining presents unique problems for miners due to the amount of CPUs able to run per rig. Both space and additional hardware per rig means the Return on Investment (ROI) is typically longer than other hardware.

FPGA: Field Programmable Gate Arrays have multiple uses outside of mining but don't share the consumer availability of GPUs and CPUs. FPGAs are the middle ground between ASICS, GPU and CPU mining. They support multiple algorithms, have resale value and provide good efficiency. However, the barrier to entry is going to be the miner's knowledge of computers in general, along with the availability deters a majority of miners.

Every hardware option requires software to start hashing. Sometimes referred to as a miner, the software can be confused with the owner of the hardware. Each piece of hardware requires different types of software. ASICS will typically run proprietary software with open source being scarce. GPU and CPU mining, however, can run on multiple operating systems including Linux, Mac and Windows. Most miners choose to use specially designed operating systems for mining including ETHOS, HIVEOS and simple mining. When starting out, hobby miners use Windows with easily obtainable software downloaded from places like GitHub.

Mining requires a lot of hardware to complete the work sent from the Blockchain. This brings us to pools - another piece of software run by various miners to combine the hash power of multiple miners into one. When mining to a pool, the miner will submit shares. Shares are a portion of the work completed to the rest of the miners on the pool. The pool's goal is to find a block before another miner. Once found, the amount of cryptocurrency earned will be divided among the miners participating based on their shares. The upside of pool mining is the regular and predictable revenue, with the downside being not earning the entire block reward.

Block reward is the amount of a particular coin paid out to miners for solving a block. For example, a block of Bitcoin is one-megabyte worth of Bitcoin transactions. The block reward is determined by the network and changes in events known as halving. When the block halves, the reward is reduced typically in half. This means that miners must take into account changes in reward versus price of the coin itself. Once the miner has found a block or received a payout from the pool in the currency they are mining, they must exchange for fiats to cover operational costs.

As earlier emphasized, the primary cost of mining is power. So typically, miners will pull enough out to pay their power bill. To facilitate these transactions, miners use various exchanges depending on the region.

Trading Bitcoin

Bitcoin trading is an instrument for making profit in the short term. Before delving into the Bitcoin market, it is important that you make a valid decision to either become an investor or a Trader. For investors, they purchase Bitcoin and hold on for a specific period hoping that the value of Bitcoin will appreciate in order to yield profit. It is usually a long-term profit solution.

Meanwhile, traders focus on short-term profit, meaning they purchase Bitcoin and utilize the volatility of the market to sell in and out of trades. Basically, it goes down to the 'Buy Low, Sell High'. Most individuals like to become a mixture of both.

The Bitcoin market is very volatile and as such, it is not uncommon to witness over 40% swings in the market every single day. If you are on the right side of the trade you can identify openings that allow you to make quick profits. However, being on the wrong side will only lead to lots of loss in quick succession. It is up to you to evaluate what your goals are and the level of risks you are willing to take.

Trading Bitcoin with Coinbase/Bittrex

There are different ways to trade Bitcoin but one of the easiest places to buy and sell Bitcoin is Coinbase. Coinbase has been on the map for a very long time and it is regarded as the most reliable and trusted source to get Bitcoin. To trade with Coinbase, simply log on to coinbase.com and sign up for an account. Next, you will have to go through a verification process to verify your identity, so don't be alarmed if it is demanding for personal information.

Once you have been verified and have linked up your bank account or your credit card, you can now go ahead to buy your Bitcoin. Aside Bitcoin, Coinbase also offers Ethereum, Litecoin, and Bitcoin Cash, so you have options to choose from.

To purchase Bitcoin, click the Bitcoin option and select "Buy". From there, you can select how much Bitcoin you would like to purchase.

Once you have made the decision to trade your Bitcoin, you would be required to transfer the coins to an exchange. Imagine the exchange in the form of a stock market where you have a brokerage account allowing you to purchase shares of companies. In the Bitcoin case, however, you are purchasing coins. There are several different exchanges that you can use which have the best reliability as well as a seamless user experience. An example is Bittrex, which is regarded as the next-generational currency exchange.

When you log on to the exchange's website, create and account, fill in your details and verify your identity. Once you are on your account, access your wallet to choose which coin you want to deposit into the exchange. Move over to the deposit icon and click on it.

Your wallet address instantly appears. Copy the entire wallet address, backtrack to Coinbase, and select the Send tab. Next you select how much you want to send and paste in your wallet address (double-check the wallet address again). Once you have that paste in, you can go ahead and click send. Note that the transfer of Bitcoin could take minutes before processing.

Once you have the Bitcoin available on the exchange, you can go to the exchange market and choose the coin you would like to trade. There are over a thousand cryptocurrency to trade. It is pertinent that you make your research on the most valuable coin to trade. Once you select the coins market, you will be presented with some charts, your buy and sell books and the transaction history. This is where you go ahead and place your order.

If you want to purchase a coin and its current price, you can select the price and click buy.

However, most professional advice that you initiate buy order below the asking price. Once this is done, your order will be placed in the order books, as you await verification.

It is advisable to remove your coin off of the exchange once you have purchased, and transfer it to your actual wallet. As it stands Coinbase only provides a market for about 50 cryptocurrencies. If you are purchasing a different coin not listed on Coinbase, you are definitely going to need a wallet. The best way to do that is to access the official website of that coin and use whatever the recommended wallet is. The next phase totally depends on whether you want to keep your coins much longer or trade in and out.

Trading Bitcoin with Binance

Binance is one of the topmost cryptocurrency trading platforms that offer unlimited coins and options. Binance offers some of the newest and highly prospective cryptocurrencies currently evolving that you cannot purchase through traditional means such as Coinbase.

The first step is to open a Binance account, set your account/ deposit and select a product/coin to trade, otherwise known as a currency pair. When you trade currencies, you have to trade in pairs because a purchase of a currency means that you have to sell another.

To buy Bitcoin, locate the BTC/USDT icon, which translates to Bitcoin against the US Dollar Tether. The USDT is a cryptocurrency that is supposed to follow the US Dollar in value one for one. This means that whatever the value of the US Dollar is compared to Bitcoin, the USTD will follow that exactly. The USTD is particularly useful in transferring fiat currency into the market to trade against Bitcoin.

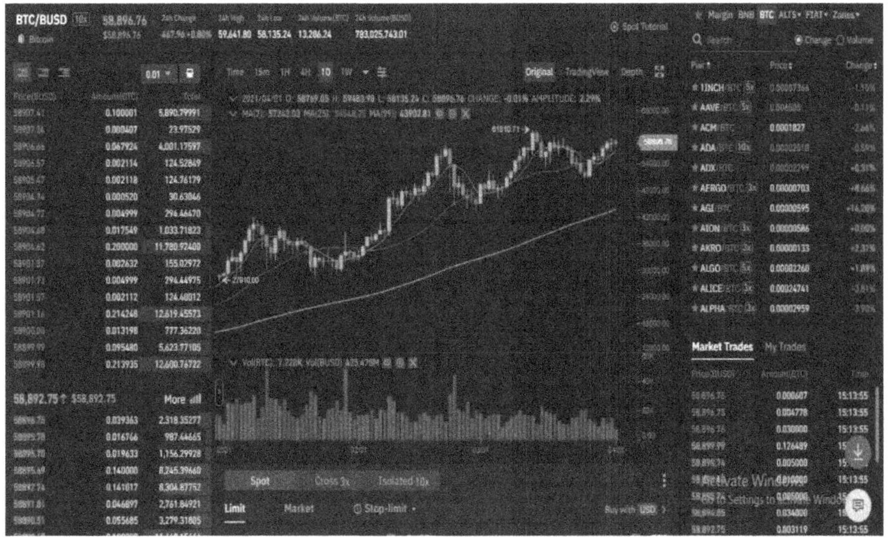

On the Bitcoin icon (BCT) tab, you are given the leverage to trade other currencies against Bitcoin. For instance, when you click on ETH/BTC, it means that you would be buying Ethereum and selling Bitcoin. The reason for this is that coins must be traded in pairs. It relatively means that the coin you are buying will outperform the sold coin. Additionally, you can buy any of the coins with fiat currency (buying Bitcoin against the US Dollar, for example).

One of basic features of Binance is a graph known as the candlestick chart. The lines in green are the upward movement of a coin for that period, while the red line is a downward price movement for that period. You can also access a specific time frame to view the chart and monitor price movement. The bottom of the candlestick graph indicates the lowest price for that period, while the top indicates the highest price for the same period. At the end of that period, the candlestick will be made.

When initiating buy on Binance, your request is placed in the order book. The order book is a book of trades and orders, which allows you to see every single order in the market. The red numbers are sellers, while the green numbers are buyers. Buyers will always be below sellers because the sellers want to sell their stock or currency at a high price and buyers or bidders want to buy at a low price.

As a beginner, the spot market is the one that you should trade. It is easy and devoid of the complex futures, derivatives and borrowed money. At the top section, you will notice the current price of Bitcoin against the US Dollar and the changes it has made in the last 24 hours. This gives you an idea of where the trading range is for that day as well as the trading volume.

CHAPTER FIVE

Understanding Tokens - Initial Coin Offering (ICO)

A token is a placeholder for a future value or a product or service. Think of it like a $50 gift card that is available on eBay for $30. That gift card is just a piece of plastic, however, if used at the store for what it is intended for, you can exchange that value for something material. There are three types of tokens, which include Currency, Utility and Investment Asset.

Currency tokens are tokens that promise future value by exchanging your token for the cryptocurrency once the project is finished. For example, when the Ethereum platform was first proposed, you could buy an Ethereum token for 18 cents. Currently, Ethereum coins are valued for more than $200 each.

On the other hand, a utility token is built to provide investors with something other than money. For example, many cryptocurrency exchange platforms offer tokens to their investors and those tokens are used to reduce the transaction fees for people trading on their platform that hold their tokens. It has no monetary value but you get a discount from using them.

Lastly, the investment assets token is very similar to a stock or equity in a company. These tokens are acquired through a process called a Security Token Offering (STO), which represents tradable financial assets. This is the most secure way of getting a token for investors because it is more regulated and prevents frauds from occurring.

After Bitcoin gained world-renowned status by hitting $20,000, many companies began forming their own tokens to achieve that same status. They offered them to people for investment through a process called an Initial Coin Offering (ICO).

Initial Coin Offering (ICO)
An ICO is a phenomenon that emerged from crowdfunding, allowing new cryptocurrencies and Blockchain technology companies to release their own cryptocurrency with the sole aim of funding. The company might exchange their cryptocurrency for Bitcoins or fiat currency. It uses the crowdsourced capital to continue to grow its technology, while both the company and investors have an incentive to see the cryptocurrency grow.

ICOs did not exist until a few years ago. The first ICO is typically attributed to Mastercoin. In 2013, the cryptocurrency managed to raise over 5 million Dollars in Bitcoin through the sale of their Mastercoin token. Later followed were Ethereum and Wave, raising 18 million and 16 million Dollars respectively. These paved the way for other companies to efficiently kick-start cryptocurrency projects.

ICO is an unregulated way to crowdfund for a cryptocurrency startup without going through The Securities and Exchange Commission (SEC). Basically, these companies have an idea for a cryptocurrency and they crowd fund the fund to start the business through an ICO. Once the project is done and live, those tokens are converted into cryptocurrency.

A particular feature of the ICOs is that it is a medium via which entrepreneurs raise funds for their new cryptocurrency projects. They do this without having to go through the regular traditional fundraising procedures or solutions from banks or other financial institutions.

At the initial phase, the startup company provides a unique and structured plan where they present detailed information of everything that might be interesting and relevant for potential investors to be aware of. The presentation or document is referred to as a White Paper. There is a clear target of the amount of money needed to be raised within a specific time frame in order for the project to take place. In case this target is not met, the money should be returned to the investors. If the target is reached, however, then the company utilizes it to initiate the new cryptocurrency system.

During the ICO process or campaign, the company sells its tokens, which work in a similar way to shares of a public company, which are sold to investors in an Initial Public Offering (IPO). Although, ICOs work much like IPOs, the key difference here is that you are not buying a share of ownership, but a unit for the project. Even though the token is tied to the company's value, it is not regarded as an actual share. Secondly, it is unlike an IPO where only certain people can participate and that requires a large amount of paperwork regulated by the government to function.

Individuals who buy this token are early adopters who believe in the success of the project, in what may lead to a significant increase in value of the currency that they hold. In the long run, they will be able to sell the coins for a profit. Alternatively, they can keep holding the cryptocurrency for an even higher value in the future.

Creating a new cryptocurrency starts out through an ideation process where an entrepreneur thinks that they have an amazing idea for the creation of a new and revolutionary cryptocurrency. This requires the need for a company, a great team and a long-term vision. However, the most vital requirement to creating a new crypto is funds. An entrepreneur is often left with the option of approaching banks and venture capital firms, where they need to deal with all kinds of paperwork and regulations, and even giving up on some of the legal rights of the project.

Alternatively, the entrepreneur opts for ICOs. After creating the White Paper, the company then sets up a standard website. The main objective of the website is to convince potential investors of the project's long-term success. As an investor, you receive coins of the new cryptocurrency, hoping for a significant rise in value following the official launch.

One of the most interesting features of ICOs is that during the ICO process, there are different stages where the currencies are sold for different prices. At the beginning, the tokens are sold at the cheapest price, the closer they get to the targeted time frame, the price rises higher. After this, the price also begins to change once they start being traded on cryptocurrency exchanges. These changes sometimes create great opportunities for profits at the right entry and exit moment.

Meanwhile, an ICO is decentralized and is able to adopt just about anyone in participation. The decentralized state means that ICOs come with far more risks. Although there are great opportunities embedded, the legitimacy of the company is not always certain.

In 2017, there were companies releasing their ICOs and some white paper with fabricated business marketing to the public, getting their attention and having people invest their money into the project. After the ICO was launched, the project developer took all of that and absconded. During this time, people and investors lost billions of Dollars and made a very bad name for the cryptocurrency space.

After this period in 2017, the SEC cracked down on these listings of ICOs. Due to the fact that these ICOs are unregulated they do not have to go through the process that the SEC requires to have equities in companies. Google and Facebook both blocked the ability to run ads on ICOs.

At that point, the SEC offered these cryptocurrency companies the option to run an STO. This is very similar to a standard company's IPO. The STO is an easier process than an IPO but it still goes through the regulatory standards that the SEC has. For instance, the SEC vets the company to ensure that they are legitimate business. They also required that investors hold on to their tokens for an extended period after the initial STO. This prevents a lot of pumps and dumps schemes that are often experienced.

If you want to invest in a new cryptocurrency startup and they have an ICO, run a proper research before investing into them. On the other hand, if the company is releasing an ICO, you already have the security and knowledge that it is being governed by the SEC in the United States. It is also advisable to do research on the company to see if they will be successful because that is the determining factor.

Cryptocurrency Pump-and-Dump
Pump-and-dump refers to a procedure where a single user or small groups of users try to make a lot of money off an asset (stocks or coins) by pumping it. Pumping in this case means that they are going to buy a ton of the asset. Cryptocurrency pump and dump schemes vary in their methods. Although, pre-mined coins ICOs and other methods were used within potential pump and dump schemes.

The scheme is simply the promotion of a product (cryptocurrency coins), after insiders have made a low position. After promotion of the coin, followers rush to invest and grab the immediate opportunity posted on any message board, including the social media space. The co9n is then sold by insiders at an inflated rate for profit, while those who bought the coin during the promotion phase are left holding the bag for low value or worst-case scenario, for value-less coins.

The chart below portrays a classic example of a pump-and-dump. As the chart shows, the group will start loading on stock, then begin the promotion phase. With a promotion phase, the schemers start to sell their shares, once they see a rapid price increase, as others begin to become bagholders of the stock of cryptocurrency. Once the group starts to sell their stock or coins, panic selling ensues and investors become bagholders.

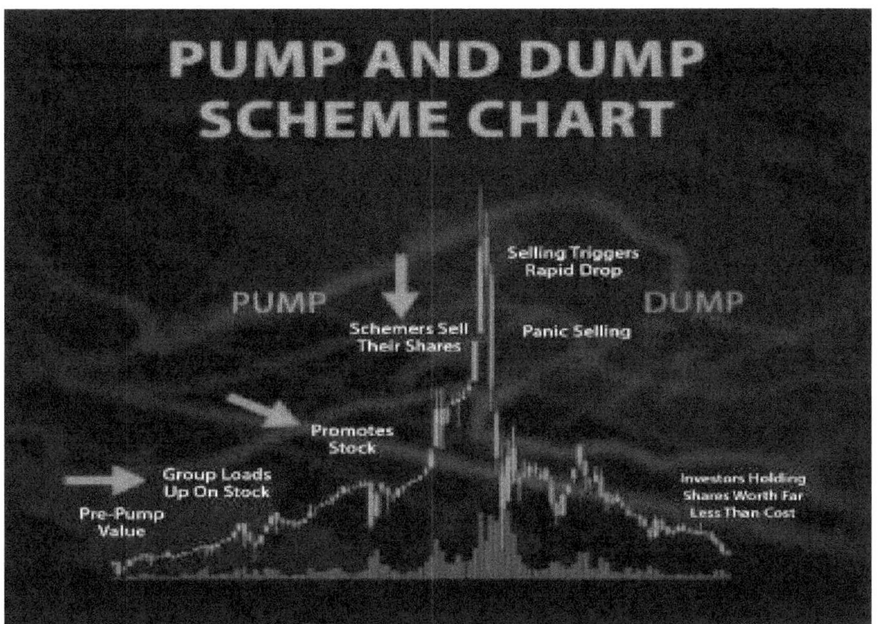

Foremost pump-and-dump trader, Wulong became the first to draft a comprehensive analysis on how pump and dump market manipulation worked. With a seven-step process on how to stage a pump-and-dump successfully, Wulong was known for manipulating Dogecoin from 50 Satoshis to about 190 Satoshis – the very first pump and dump of Dogecoin in 2015.

According to the analysis, what this tool was seven steps to achieve it: Position Building; Price Suppression; Testing the Pump; The Actual Pump; Shakeouts; Relocation and Distribution; The Dump also known as exiting. Keep in mind that these steps are not for traditional investors with limited funds but for those who can mandate the market individually or more than likely as a group of investors with a big pool of money or cryptocurrencies. These investors are commonly called Whales.

Whales in the scheme are regarded as traders with significant bankrolls that heavily impact the markets direction. The purpose is to get a grasp of how to manipulate the market and trade in shadows, and then profit from that understanding. One of the tools Whales use as defined by Wulong is market volume. This refers to a number of units traded during a period.

Whales contribute to about 80% to 70% of the volume seen on the market. This is enough to alter the direction of the market. Volume is important to understanding this method, as market volume will be used as an indicator for health of the coin with a popularity of trades. It should be noted that some individuals and algorithm traders will use volume as an important indicator of a big market. A spike of high volume trade will usually either indicate a pump or dump within the market.

Position Building: As the first step in this strategy, this is the stage, which requires a substantial amount of share to work on the pumps. One of the most practicable methods is the use of micro-buys. Through buys in relative small amounts, it avoids price scaling and also masks the existence of whales. Some alternative coins, however, have low volumes and will take donkey years to build positions through micro buys. In such cases, whales will be forced to do a pump to encourage sellers. Doge to Bitcoin has been one of the examples of this step.

Price Suppression: This stage is done after piles of all coins are purchased to overwhelm prices as long as it can by utilizing sell walls to buy more cheaply. Sell walls are enough to appear like the invisible hand of the market – minor supply and demand.

Test Pump: Test pump is used for whales to test and ensure control of the market. This may happen throughout pumps and dumps. By running a test pump, you get an idea of where resistance falls next and how many weak hands are in the market will be given. Wulong specifically states that whales distaste weak hands, as they do not give support during a pump. Therefore, test pumps will be used to get rid of investors in the early stage.

The Actual Pump: This is performed once the weak hands have been forced out.

The Shakeouts: Within the pump phase, shakeouts will be used to drive prices so low that the prices will go below the whales' buying price. Although this would intentionally be at a loss, shakeouts intentionally simulate a dump to cause despair within the market. Weak hands traders will usually exit the market at this point even at a loss.

Reallocation and Distribution: Sometimes during a pump, buying into their own walls, whales will have more of the coin than expected. If this is the case, prices are dropped once the whales sell their coins into the market. However, this is not enough to cause alarm for a dump. For example if the coin was distributed at $5 per coin, prices will be driven down to $450. Whales will know that traders will want to leave at a profit and the price difference from the buy originally at $5 is not a significant amount of loss at $450. So they carefully distribute their coins without causing huge loss to the market.

The Dump: After all stages have been completed, the final stage begins. The dump is where the whales take their profit, completely exiting from the market. Exiting strategies vary. Although, the most common idea everyone might have is that whale micro sell or massively dump into buy walls. These are just basic exiting strategies and are not the most profitable methods. One method Wulong stated is exiting during a pump, which works by having sell walls in place and buying into these walls time and again, until there is enough crowd to follow. Once they follow, they will buy into the whales' sell walls. This allows the whales to exit portion bit by bit until they finally exit the market.

Cryptocurrency Terms and Slangs
HODL

This acronym is one of the most common slangs in the cryptocurrency space, usually associated with long term investors. As one of the critical philosophies of crypto investment, HODL means "Hold On for Dear Life". It occurs when investors hold on to their cryptocurrency for the long term and pay no attention to the short-term price action. People who HODL are referred to as HODLERS and some who follow this route intend to hold on to their Bitcoin or any other cryptocurrency until that single currency is worth millions. Alternatively, some HODLERS intend to HODL until cryptocurrency becomes a globally accepted financial phenomenon without any restrictions.

By contrast people who cannot handle huge swings to the upside or downside and sell instead, are referred to as weak hands. Most weak hands are retail investors who are new to cryptocurrency. HODL was first used on the Bitcoin talk forum in December 2013, when a user game drunkenly posted about missing the top Bitcoin's first Bull Run. The misspelt post "I am Hodling" quickly became a meme, with respondent saying that they too will be hodling their Bitcoin instead of actively trading it. HODL is most often used when the price of Bitcoin or some other crypto suddenly drops or spikes. So when someone asks you if you are selling your Bitcoin when it reaches all-time highs, respond politely but firmly that you are "hodling".

FOMO

This means "Fear of Missing Out". In the context of cryptocurrency, FOMO is what you feel when you see the price of a coin or token you do not have pushing past new all-time highs. Interestingly, FOMO is technically a social anxiety, which was identified over 25 years ago by marketing strategist Dr. Dan Herman. In 2004, Author and Venture Capitalist, Partrick McGinnis, popularized the acronym in one of his publications – an OP-ED - at the Harvard Kennedy Business School.

Widespread FOMO is also considered by many to be the second last stage of a bull market cycle. This is why you would come across a lot of discussions around retail and institutional FOMO when it comes to talking about what is going to drive Bitcoin to an all-time high during a bull market. In fact, some believe that measuring this FOMO is how you can time the top of a bull market and this can easily be done by searching terms like cryptocurrency and buying Bitcoin on Google search trends.

Bagholder

The term bag refers to holding of cryptocurrencies or other tokens in the portfolio by the investor. Generally, a bagholder is an investor who keeps hold of investments and assets regardless of a continuous dip in the value of the asset. Also, this may turn out to be an event where the asset may become worthless, yet hoping with time for market recovery in the future. With this, the bagholder knows the risk involved in losing some or all investments or assets during the persistence of a downward trend. The bagholder is also said to be someone who HODL.

Most investors are unaware of the strategies involved in the market before delving in. There is often a consensus among bagholders that their bag may increase in value and yield more profit in the future. In cases like this, bagholders are often not available to analyze the performance of their assets in the market. Consisting of a situation wherein the investor is not aware of the underperforming coiner asset in the market, then we have the disposition effect that can be referred to human psychology. This effect describes an investor who intentionally chooses to hold the bag with less value. Against this backdrop, the investor sells off the bag whose value has experienced a slight increase, while hoping for a much-needed recovery.

MCAP

This refers to Market Capitalization or Market Cap for short and it is an important metric in cryptocurrency. It is used to rank coins by the amount invested in them and determine which coins have the most universal support. For instance, the largest market cap holder is said to be Bitcoin. This is why it is referred to as the world's largest cryptocurrency. Ethereum and Ripple's XRP follows Bitcoin in rankings based on their market caps.

To determine an individual cryptocurrency's market cap, you simply need to multiply the coins current circulating supply by its price. The current number of coins is the circulating supply, which have been mined excluding any coins that may be locked up in any way. In other words, circulating supply is the total number of coins in existence and that are technically accessible and available to traders and investors.

Shitcoin

Sometimes it is quite evident that you are dealing with a grade A Shitcoin. Unhatched Podcast host, Ruben Samson is credited with defining what a Shitcoin is. He refers to a Shitcoin as a coin that has the potential to further dip as a result of its defective fundamentals. According to him, the originators and early adopters of the coin mislead the market with constant denial of how valueless the coin is so as to set new investors up for losses and reap from their investments.

In November 2010, the term Shitcoin was first used by a few investors who had thought that the success of Bitcoin will bring about a lot of get rich quick imitators in the crypto market and Shitcoins have not failed to live up to expectation. There are actually two literal Shitcoins noted on Ether scan as ERC20 tokens and the FTX cryptocurrency exchange also offers a number of Shitcoin index tokens that allow you to long or short a basket of 58 altcoins. All Shitcoins are destined to become either dead coins or zombie coins.

CHAPTER SIX

TRADING SECRETS AND STRATEGIES

The cryptocurrency market is undoubtedly filled with lots of uncertainties and volatilities. Traders are always urged to carefully analyze the market before delving in. In light of this, traders adopt different strategies and techniques in a bid to beat the market and make huge profits. Which one works, depend on a few factors including your forbearance for risk, commitment and so on. At the end, the onus lies on the circumstances of individuals.

There is no one size fits all in terms of trading cryptocurrencies. Remember that it is very pertinent to do your research properly before exploring the market. Also never, invest more than you are willing to lose.None of these tactics is foolproof and there is a certain amount of risk associated with any kind of trading.

Furthermore, trading tactics are specific or rather iconic to certain individuals and may not be generalized. For the avoidance of doubt, this chapter will look specifically at some of the best, proven and popularly acquainted trading strategies with a high number of success stories.

'Hodling' Strategy: As earlier discussed, to hodl means to buy a sum of cryptocurrency and store it securely safely for potential long-term growth. Here, we are referring to keeping your digital coins until it increases in value. Hodling is a pretty basic strategy which involves buying assets and keeping them safe for the long-term, till they probably hit your expected value outcome. For many who are astute cryptocurrency investors, it has been very effective, especially when you consider Bitcoin's meteoric rise in value since it was launched. Other cryptocurrencies are also following suit and have also been experiencing a huge rise in value, especially Ethereum and Litecoin.

Inversely, the 'hodling' strategy also comes with its own risks. If you don't mark entry points and the market drops, you can only cut your losses or wait and watch. This can be an awkward and frightening situation because you could lose all of your investments and gains in one sitting, especially when you are not monitoring trade. This scenario is why experts often advise that traders and investors only put into the market what they can afford to lose.

Dollar Cost Averaging: This is a variation of 'hodling 'your cryptocurrency that militates against the risks of trading your coins. The goal with this strategy is to make regular investments repeated intervals, possibly of the same amount. Regardless of the day-to-day price, this strategy gives you average overall price.

For instance, if you make a plan to buy $50 each month from the first day of the month, and stick to that regardless of what happens to the price, it does not matter if the date that you choose falls on a weekend or a bank holiday. Of course, cryptocurrency markets are open 24 /7. This strategy verges against the movement of major market trends and runs through a long-term position and time frame. This invariably helps in keeping track of the market trends. It is also arguably one of the best strategies available.

Day Trading: This tactics is specifically for those who are willing to stick to their screen and monitor trading movements and are envisaging more short-term gains. Unlike the Holding strategies, this offers more nuances and possibly a better deal. However, if you are going to stick to day trading you should be able to put in more shifts and hours. Day trading focuses solely on the buying of cryptocurrency in what you believe will be a higher or lower price. This also anticipates short-term movements, which means that the amount of profit you are set to make depends on the movement of price in your favor – upward or downward price trend. At any point, you could sell your investment for a profit.

One of the downsides of this strategy or seeming risk is that the price of an asset may negatively beat your expectations. The day aspect of Day Trading, relates to the short-term nature of the position you take. What this implies is that you set your trading positions within a time frame. This presumably may take up to a certain number of hours or day as against 'hodling', which may take months or years. Depending on your preference, you could choose to trade at night or a specific period suitable for you.

Swing Trading: Swing trading requires an astronomical level of patience where you affirm your positions until you notice a trend in the market. It is also a strategy applied you're your predicted swing runs its course or you notice a sign of reversal. Unlike the aforementioned strategy, swing trading requires less time and attention. On the other hand, you are mandated to get a hold of the trends the moment they form. The time spent on holding may be used to permit a positive shift in price, resulting in higher profits. Also, the price of the market swings the other way or against your trade, resulting in huge loss if you have invested much in.

Scalp Trading: This is the opposite form of swing trading where you mount your position in the market for much shorter periods, specifically in seconds or minutes. If you are expecting much gain in this trading system, then you may likely not get it. In scalp trading, the gains you make are way smaller and you are expected to give the market a more focused attention. Here, your cryptocurrency can pile up because they can make so many trades per day. Swing trading has the potential to be more profitable in the short-term than the longer-term strategies.

Technical Analysis - Understanding Charts and Patterns

Ardent traders are always on the lookout for some of the best ways to maximize the cryptocurrency market. While this is no easy task, technical analysis of the crypto market can help you build formations that would fine-tune the way you pick up trends and ultimately trade your currencies. Technical Analysis may look scary and complicated but the truth is that it is not.

Your ability to use technical analysis in order to make good trading decisions and inevitably make money in the cryptocurrency market is imperative If you do not understand the key details in technical analysis, particularly studying patterns and charts, it could lead to aimless trading and unavoidable loss of money as trader or you would struggle to make profits overtime.

In the crypto market, Technical Analysis can be referred to as the study of historic price movements in order to make accurate decisions of what the market may do next. This means that there are steps taken in making accurate decisions regarding price movements in the market. Every part of technical analysis is based on price. Price trends are nothing more than higher highs and higher lows or lower lows and lower highs in price. Trends like structure, suppose and resistance as well as indicators are all formulas added to historic price data in order to plot that indicator on your charts.

Candlestick Charts

The core of any trading market is the candlestick chart. What a candlestick represents on a chart is the price movement throughout a certain period, depending on the time frame that you are on – the daily chart. For instance, if you are on a 5 min chart, each of the candlesticks will represent five minutes of price movement.

Candlesticks are represented by two parts, which include the Body and the Wick. Using the aforementioned time frame, a green candle represents a five-minute period where the price of an asset went up or closed above where it opened. On the other hand, the red candle represents a five-minute period where the price closed below or went lower during the time frame.

The opening of a green candle is where it opened during the time frame. For instance, if the opening of a candle is at 12:00, what the candle will represent is the open of a candle at the time, while the low would be the lowest point the price got to during the specified time frame. Correspondingly, the high would be the highest point the price of an asset got to during a five-minute window and the close would occur 12:05. This means that the current price at this time would be the ending price during a five-minute period.

For the red candle, we would have an opening at the top of the body as a result of the closing of price or that time it went lower during a five-minute window. The highest point on a red candle is the top or wick of the candle, which translates to the highest point price, got to within the time frame. The low, on the flip side, is the lowest wick on the candle, while the close is the closing price after minutes of data on a five-minute chart (opening at 12:00 and closing at 12:05). The candlestick shows you all of the action of price along a specific time frame.

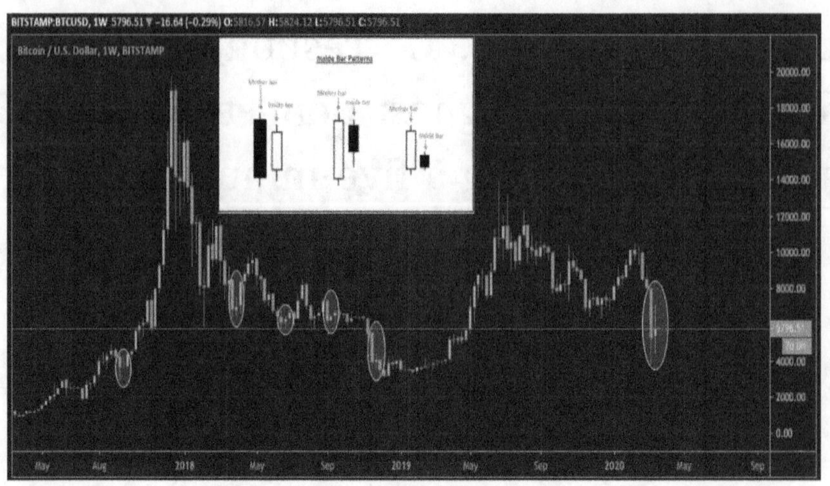

A large amount of candles are put together in order to interpret what the price of an asset is most likely to do next identifying trends and areas of value as well as entry patterns. Each candle represents 24 hours of price movement. On an actual chart, a green candle represents a day where price went higher or a day where the price closed above where it opened. A red candle, on the other hand, represents a day where price went lower or a day where price closed below where it opened.

Trending Markets

In the trend markets, there are significant aspects identified as the uptrend and downtrend. The uptrend is nothing more than when a candlestick chart is consistently making new highs and then higher lows. The reason for utilizing a trend market is because it gives your trade more accuracy and as such, most traders gravitate towards the trend market. Trends markets can make up for better rewards to risk setups. It is an easier and safer bet to ride a trend that is already dominant than to pick the top or bottom of a market trying to trade reversals. In light of this, it is most preferable to trade with the trend.

To identify trends, it is best to take note of impulsive moves in a trend market. This refers to the big moves that break into new highs. After an impulsive move, the market takes a breather, which is regarded as pullbacks. The most objective way to identify these trends is that the lowest low of the pullback cannot be broken for a trader to stay in an uptrend. An uptrend market is considered to be on a high, until you break the close below the lowest low of the previous pullback.

Indicators

Trading indicators are formulas added to current and historic price and mathematical equations in order to plot lines and histograms on your chart. The purpose of trading indicators is to help simplify what price is doing. For instance, a candlestick chart itself can be very confusing at times, so trading indicators are meant to clean up some of the complexities. Indicators can also be used as an invaluable object rule in a trading strategy or in any form of trading, to help create a more consistent trade. Essentially, trading indicators can help to provide clarity on market conditions as well as identify trends, areas of values, find entry points and determine where you want to place your stops and targets.

There are thousands of trading indicators in the cryptocurrency space, but the most proven and useful indicator is the ATR Indicator. ATR stands for Average True Range. It is a strategy that gives you the average moment of price out of the last 14 candles. The way it works is that it adds up the price movement in total – the total amount of pips. Each candle moved out of the last fourteen candles is divided by fourteen to give you the total average moment of price in the last fourteen candles. Note that any trading platform should have an ATR indicator. Traders often bemoan loss of money to trades, despite having a good reward to risk ratio. With the ATR Indicator, you can stay in line with the volatility of a market currency pair or time frame.

Candlestick Patterns

Candlestick patterns are candlesticks that form in a very specific way in order to help us determine what price is likely to do next. The shooting star candle, hammer pattern, engulfing pattern are all lists of Candlestick patterns used by traders. Candlestick patterns can be used to help traders detect reversals and provide clarity on market sentiment. Additionally, these patterns can be used for entry reasons, trend continuation and reversal trades. Candlestick patterns also form between one and a few candles.

Chart Patterns

Unlike the candlestick pattern, the chart pattern forms between ten to about fifty candles. They are identifiable patterns that can give traders an indication of possible reversals and market sentiment. They also point out possible entries in the market and help elevate your trading game. For most traders, chart patterns are easier ways to enter trades. Double tops and double bottoms are revered as the most proven charts patterns. In these patterns, there are needs for objective rules. Chart patterns indicate a market that sloops, creates a level of support, and then bounces up to a level of resistance.

Cryptocurrency Risk Assessment

Getting into the cryptocurrency space can be an exciting journey. Nevertheless, tread with caution; it takes a lot of time and assessment to hit Gold. The cryptocurrency market should not be underestimated or treated with levity. Here are some of the risk assessments you should make before trading or investing your hard-earned money:

Consider Listing: before taking a dive into a cryptocurrency projector or the utility of the token, you want to invest in, keenly ensure that the token is listed on a number of trusted exchanges or at least in five of the topmost exchanges available to lots of investors and traders. Listing is a crucial part of the cryptocurrency space due to two main reasons:

Firstly, exchanges can get hacked. In the event that an exchange gets heavily hacked there is a huge possibility that it would lead to bankruptcy. The exchange would have no other choice but to close up shop – so many crypto enthusiasts have experienced this with Cryptopia. Cryptopia was offering the largest listing of altcoins when it was functional. After it was invaded and hacked, most of the tokens listed lost lots of value, while others went into extinction – they could not be bought or sold.

Additionally, we have seen scenarios where exchanges liquidate due to lack of profits in the crypto business. Exchanges can close simply because they do not have enough money to support their expenses. A critical example of this development is that of Coinexchange, a once vast cryptocurrency exchange in China. Coinexchange did not experience a hack but it packed up for another reason – the exchange failed to make enough money to sustain itself. The results are the same as the previous scenario. Another candid instance of these two consequences is Metrix Coin. This cryptocurrency was doomed to fail not because of the nature of the project, but because it was listed on Cryptopia and Coinexchange. When the exchanges closed, this crypto was delisted and as a result, lost all of its value.

Liquidity: One of the vital risk assessments to make is to ensure that the cryptocurrency you want to invest in has a very good daily volume. Let's say you have about $10,000 to invest, you need to select a cryptocurrency that has at least $100,000 in daily volume. This is in order to get a good resale value.

When you are ready to sell it off with a profit, your order will be filled easily. As proven, the best practice is to choose a cryptocurrency with a huge daily volume, thus you are certain of filling your order whenever you want.

Weigh ICOs or Avoid Them: While they have reliable Initial Coin Offerings who offer coins on pre-sale and have proven to be trustworthy, the ICO space is becoming more of a gamble in recent times. Most of the ICOs littered around are frauds and should not be trusted. Even if you are lucky and you choose a great project, which has raised millions of Dollars, chances are that buying the ICO is never a good deal. Each time an ICO gets listed on exchanges, there seems to be a hike or peak on prices, which are essentially followed by a big drop down. As expected, this pattern continues to repeat itself, time and again. Some of the early investors could take advantage of this situation due to the fact that they are well abreast in how the game all plays out. Howbeit, if you are new to the cryptocurrency space, kindly avoid ICOs.

Longevity and Utility: In investment or trading, it is expedient that the project you are investing in has at least one year of existence in the market. Less than that will be considered as a high-risk investment. Furthermore, it is outright that you consider the utility of the crypto project. The utility of the token is defined by its use case. For instance, a crypto project has a product, which serves the needs of people in the real world; chances are that the project will last as long as the product exists.

As a vivid case study, the V chain and Wharton chain crypto projects are operating in the supply chain industry. The Basic Attention Token and Netbooks are offering new ways for browsing the web and then there is Ethereum with a smart contract serving other crypto projects. These projects all have one specific attribute associated with them: real product and real time use case.

About the Author

Sean Scott has been in and around the financial sphere for years as an expert trader and investor and financial analyst. He is a successful investor in the stock market, forex, cryptocurrency and other investment schemes. Sean has also trained a number of individuals who have had enormous accomplishments in the cryptocurrency industry.

He has an MBA in Financial Management from the University of Tennessee, Knoxville, Tennessee. He is married with two amazing kids.

www.ingramcontent.com/pod-product-compliance
Lightning Source LLC
Chambersburg PA
CBHW071247150726
48001CB00018B/399